LITTLE CITIZENS

WE FOLLOW THE RULES

THERESA EMMINIZER

PowerKiDS press

Published in 2023 by The Rosen Publishing Group, Inc.
2544 Clinton St, Buffalo, NY 14224

First Edition

Editor: Theresa Emminizer
Book Design: Rachel Rising

Photo Credits: Cover, wavebreakmedia/Shutterstock.com; pp. 4, 6, 8, 10, 12, 14, 16, 18, 20 somen/Shutterstock.com; p. 5 Inside Creative House/Shutterstock.com; p. 7 Veniamin Kraskov/Shutterstock.com; p. 9 matimix/Shutterstock.com; pp. 11 CemSelvi/iStock.com; p. 13 VGstockstudio/Shutterstock.com p. 15 Ljupco Smokovski/Shutterstock.com; pp. 17, 19 Jacob Lund/Shutterstock.com; p. 21 Littlekidmoment/Shutterstock.com.

Library of Congress Cataloging-in-Publication Data
Names: Emminizer, Theresa.
Title: We Follow the Rules / Theresa Emminizer.
Description: New York : Powerkids Press, 2023. | Series: Little Citizens | Includes glossary and index.
Identifiers: ISBN 9781538389188 (pbk.) | ISBN 9781538389201 (library bound) | ISBN 9781538389218 (ebook)
Subjects: LCSH: Citizen participation--Juvenile literature. | Rules--Juvenile literature. | Safety--Juvenile literature.
Classification: LCC BJ1631 E46 2023 | DDC 170/.83/4-dc23
Manufactured in the United States of America

CPSIA Compliance Information: Batch #CWPK23. For Further Information contact Rosen Publishing, New York, New York at 1-800-237-9932.

CONTENTS

Be a Good Citizen

You belong to a community. You're a member of your country. You're a **citizen**! Citizens have **rights**. We also have **responsibilities**. We need to think about how our actions make a difference to others. Good citizens follow the rules.

Rules Are Important

Why is it important to follow the rules? Rules give us the tools we need to get things done. They help keep us safe. They make things fairer. If nobody followed the rules, the world would be a very messy place!

Have Fun with Rules

Rules even help us have fun. Just think, without rules, we couldn't play sports! In a soccer game, all the players must follow the same rules. If one player breaks the rules, it makes the game unfair.

Rules in Action

Iris and Andy are playing a game together. But Andy isn't following the rules. Andy keeps taking extra cards. He thinks winning is more important than playing a fair game. Iris sees Andy **cheating**. It makes her mad!

Iris tells Andy she doesn't want to play with him anymore. Now Andy feels bad. He wanted to win so badly that he forgot it's not fun to play a game when someone breaks the rules. Next time, he'll follow the rules.

Stay Safe with Rules

Rules are often there to keep us safe. Wearing a seatbelt is a very important rule. So is wearing a helmet while biking. Or looking both ways before crossing the street. If we don't follow safety rules, getting hurt could be the **consequence**.

Rules in Action

It's a hot day. Bea can't wait to go for a swim! But her mom is on the phone. In Bea's family, the house rule is that nobody is allowed in the pool without a grown up to watch them.

Bea really wants to swim, but she waits. She knows it would be **dangerous** to go in the pool without her mom. When Bea's mom gets off the phone she gives her a hug. She's proud of Bea for following the rules.

Rules Rule!

Following the rules can be hard. It can be fun too! Remember that rules are there to keep us safe. You are a good citizen. You can help make your community a better place by following the rules.

GLOSSARY

cheating: Breaking the rules.

citizen: One who lives in a country legally and has certain rights.

consequence: What happens as the result of an action.

dangerous: Unsafe.

responsibility: Something a person is in charge of.

right: Something someone is allowed to have, get, or do by law.

FOR MORE INFORMATION

BOOKS

Day, Erin. *Why Do Families Have Rules?* New York, NY: PowerKids Press, 2019.

Hicks, Dwayne. *Rules in the Playground*. New York, NY: PowerKids Press, 2020.

WEBSITES

Britannica Kids
kids.britannica.com/kids/article/citizenship/399912
Read more about how you can be a better citizen!

Kid Citizen
www.kidcitizen.net/?msclkid=c45ea688d15e11ec8aa8af831090dbd2
Find out more about what it means to be a citizen!

Publisher's note to educators and parents: Our editors have carefully reviewed these websites to ensure that they are suitable for students. Many websites change frequently, however, and we cannot guarantee that a site's future contents will continue to meet our high standards of quality and educational value. Be advised that students should be closely supervised whenever they access the internet.

INDEX